Color the Proverbs

Artwork by Michal Sparks

HARVEST HOUSE PUBLISHERS
EUGENE, OREGON

Scripture quotations are from...

The New American Standard Bible®, © 1960, 1962, 1963, 1968, 1971, 1972, 1973, 1975, 1977, 1995 by The Lockman Foundation. Used by permission. (www.Lockman.org)

The New King James Version®. Copyright © 1982 by Thomas Nelson, Inc. Used by permission. All rights reserved.

The Holy Bible, New International Version®, NIV®. Copyright © 1973, 1978, 1984, 2011 by Biblica, Inc.® Used by permission. All rights reserved worldwide.

The *Holy Bible*, New Living Translation, copyright © 1996, 2004, 2007, 2013 by Tyndale House Foundation. Used by permission of Tyndale House Publishers, Inc., Carol Stream, Illinois 60188. All rights reserved.

Cover by Katie Brady Design, Eugene, Oregon

COLOR THE BIBLE is a registered trademark of The Hawkins Children's LLC. Harvest House Publishers, Inc., is the exclusive licensee of the federally registered trademark COLOR THE BIBLE.

COLOR THE PROVERBS
Copyright © 2016 by Michal Sparks
Published by Harvest House Publishers
Eugene, Oregon 97402
www.harvesthousepublishers.com

ISBN 978-0-7369-6855-3 (pbk.)

Printed in the United States of America

16 17 18 19 20 21 22 23 / VP-JC / 9 8 7 6 5 4 3 2 1

A Good Place to Begin

This coloring book is for artists of all ages and talents, and that means you! Let your creative spirit free, choose any color you like, and make each beautiful image your own. There are no rules except to have fun.

Enjoy the process. Feel free to use colored pencils, pens, watercolors, markers, and crayons—or any combination—to add color and texture to each design. Notice that all the pictures are printed on just one side of the paper. To keep colors from bleeding through to the next page, simply slip an extra piece of paper underneath the page you're working on. When finished, you might like to remove the page from the book, trim it to size, and frame your artwork for all to see.

Most importantly, have fun with the process. Enjoy experimenting with contrasting colors or different shades of the same color. Try lighter hues for a softer look, or layer and blend your colors for even more options. Allow some white space or saturate the entire piece with rich, vibrant color, depending on your mood. Let your worries go, relax in the moment, and allow your creative spirit to lead the way!

your neck, write them on the tablet of your heart.

Do not let kindness and truth leave you; bind them around

Proverbs 3:3

PROVERBS 17:17

Above all else,
guard your heart,
for everything you do
flows from it.

PROVERBS 4:23

A person finds joy in giving an apt reply

—and how good is a timely word!

Proverbs 15:23

A wise man will hear & increase in learning

Proverbs 1:5

A joyful makes a cheerful face.

Proverbs 15:13

By *wisdom* the LORD laid
the earth's foundations,
by **understanding** he set
the heavens in place;
by his *knowledge* the watery
depths were divided,
and the clouds let drop the dew.

PROVERBS 3:19-20

Like apples of gold
in settings of silver is
*a word spoken in
right circumstances.*

PROVERBS 25:11

A longing fulfilled is sweet to the soul

Proverbs 13:19

Trust in the LORD
with all your heart and
do not lean on your own
understanding. In all your
ways acknowledge Him,
and He will make your
paths straight.

PROVERBS 3:5-6

Do not forsake wisdom, and she will protect you;

love her, and she will watch over you.

Proverbs 4:6

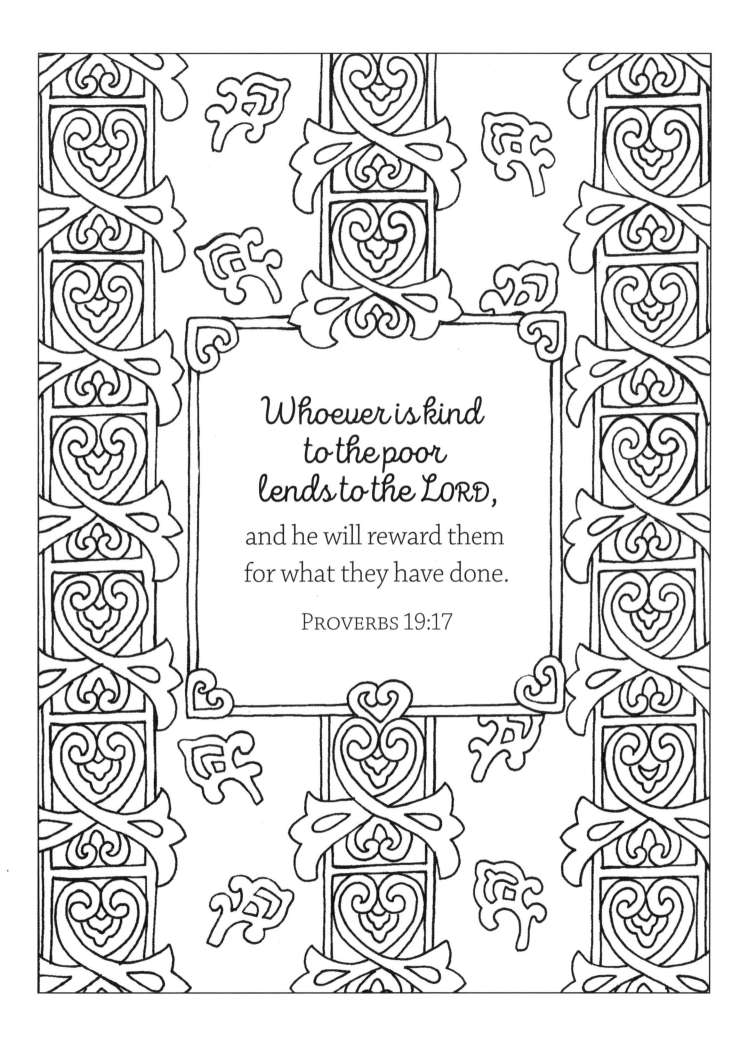

Whoever is kind
to the poor
lends to the LORD,

and he will reward them
for what they have done.

PROVERBS 19:17

She is clothed with strength and dignity;

she can laugh at the days to come.

Proverbs 31:25

As water
reflects the face,
so one's life
reflects the heart.

PROVERBS 27:19

A cheerful is good medicine.

PROVERBS 17:22

The fear of the LORD is a fountain of life

PROVERBS 14:27

Anxiety weighs down the ❤, but A kind word cheers it up.

Proverbs 12:25

As iron sharpens iron,
so one person sharpens another.

Proverbs 27:17

Blessed are those
who find wisdom,
those who gain understanding,
for she is more profitable
than silver and
yields better returns than gold.
She is more precious
than rubies;
nothing you desire can
compare with her.

PROVERBS 3:13-15

Whoever fears the LORD
has a secure fortress,
and for their children
it will be a refuge.

PROVERBS 14:26

The path of the righteous is like the morning sun, shining ever brighter till the full light of day.

Proverbs 4:18

Pleasant words are a honeycomb, sweet to the soul and healing to the bones.

Proverbs 16:24

The fruit of
the righteous
is a tree of life,
and he who
wins souls is wise.

PROVERBS 11:30

A gentle answer turns away wrath

Proverbs 15:1

The fear of the LORD is the beginning of wisdom,

and knowledge of the Holy One is understanding.

PROVERBS 9:10

How much better to
get wisdom than gold,
to get insight
rather than silver!

PROVERBS 16:16

A generous
person will prosper;
whoever refreshes others
will be refreshed.

PROVERBS 11:25

For the LORD grants wisdom!
From his mouth come
knowledge and understanding.
He grants a treasure of
common sense to the honest.
He is a shield to those
who walk with integrity.
He guards the paths of the just
and protects those
who are faithful to him.

PROVERBS 2:6-8

Hatred stirs up conflict, but love covers over all wrongs.

Proverbs 10:12

The name
of the LORD is
a strong tower;
the righteous runs
into it and is safe.

PROVERBS 18:10

The mind of man
plans his way,
but the LORD
directs his steps.

PROVERBS 16:9

By wisdom
a house is built,
and through understanding
it is established;
through knowledge its
rooms are filled with rare
and beautiful treasures.

PROVERBS 24:3-4

When you lie down,
you will not be afraid;
when you lie down,
your sleep will
be sweet.

PROVERBS 3:24

Commit to the LORD whatever you do,

and he will establish your plans.

Proverbs 16:3

A MAN of understanding holds his PEACE.

Proverbs 11:12

Better a little
with the fear of the Lord
than great wealth with turmoil.
Better a small serving of vegetables
with love than a fattened calf
with hatred.

Proverbs 15:16-17

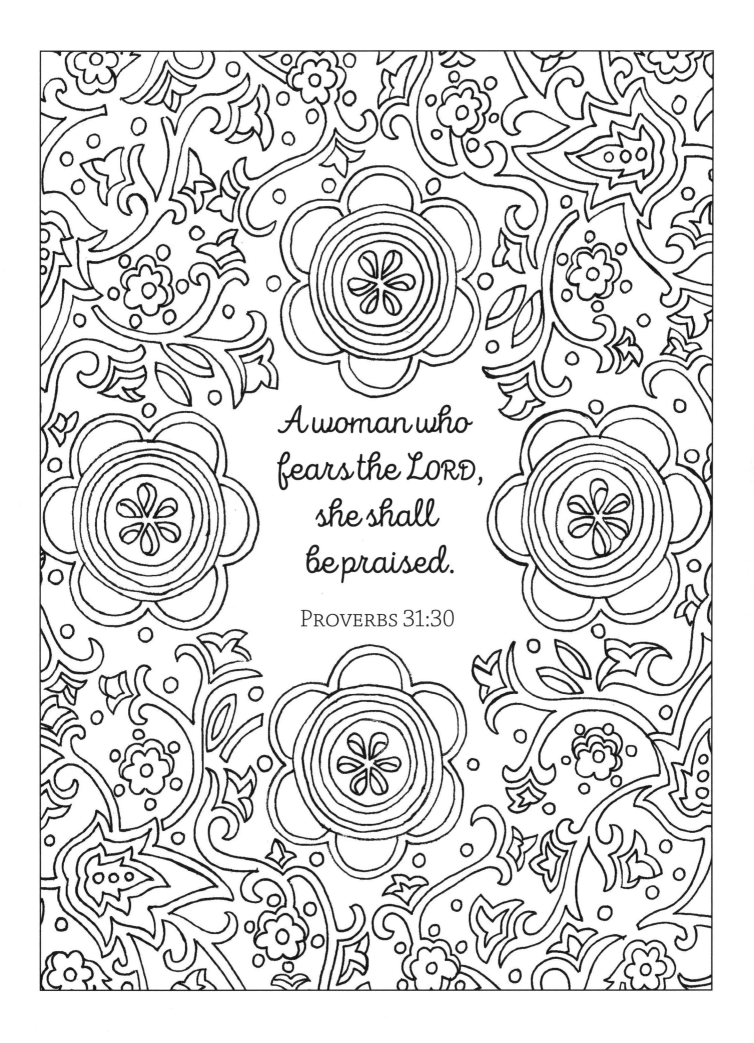

A woman who
fears the LORD,
she shall
be praised.

PROVERBS 31:30

Michal Sparks' artwork can be found throughout the home-furnishings industry in textiles, gift items, dinnerware, and more. She is the artist for *Words of Comfort for Times of Loss* and *Color the Psalms*. She and her family live in New Jersey.

We'd love to see your creations!
Share your finished projects on social media
with this hashtag:

#colorthebible

We'll be looking for your artwork!

For information on more
Harvest House coloring books for adults,
please visit our website:
www.harvesthousepublishers.com